Above and front cover: Passport photograph of James Joyce.

Back cover: Joyce at age 22.

KEY TO ULYSSES

A KEY TO THE
ULYSSES
OF JAMES JOYCE

BY

PAUL JORDAN SMITH

CITY LIGHTS

To

John Cowper Powys

WHOSE SLY MACHIAVELLIAN TAUNTS SET ME
ABOUT THE MAKING OF THIS BOOK

KEY TO BLOOM'S WANDERINGS THROUGH DUBLIN

The circles on the map on the double page spread next following indicate, roughly, Bloom's journeys throughout the day.

1. Bloom's house.
2. Post office in Westland Row.
3. Bath.
4. Route to Glasnevin Cemetery.
5. *Telegraph* office.
6. Museum (Library near-by).
7. Byrne's Pub.
8. Kiernan's.
9. Maternity hospital.
10. Night-town scene.
11. Skin-the-Goat's.
12. To Sandymount and Martello Tower.

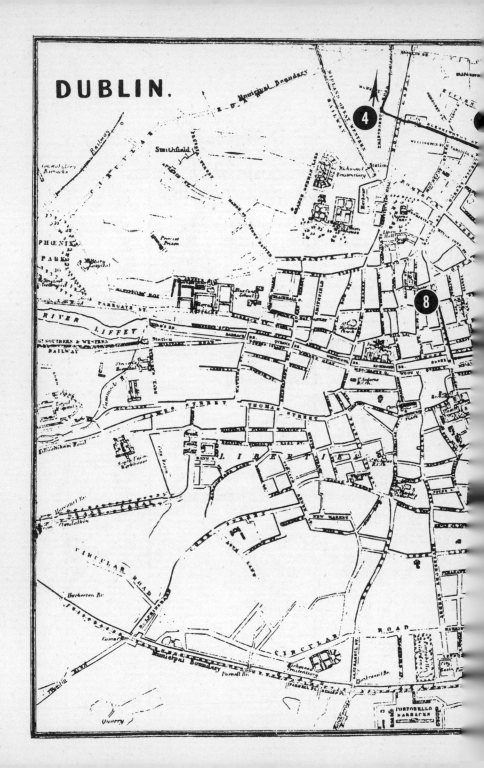

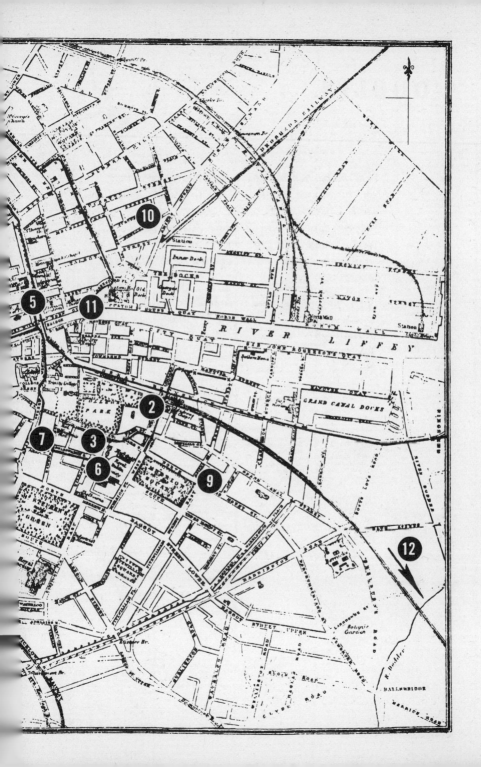

For permission to reprint one chapter contained in this volume, thanks are due to Messrs. Albert and Charles Boni. The essay, which first appeared in my On Strange Altars, has been revised and enlarged, but maintains substantially the same point of outlook there expressed.

The map of Dublin is copied from an early publication of Adam and Charles Black, Edinburgh.

CONTENTS

INTRODUCTION

THE *Ulysses* of James Joyce is, for most who
have turned its curious pages, a puzzle-book to
be gazed at and then thrown, somewhat profanely,
aside. To some it has proved a challenge; to a few
it has been a delight.

But the average novel reader expects a work of
fiction to be simple, straightforward prose. No
amount of talk about expressionism, dadaism, or
the subconscious mind, can reconcile him to the
unintelligibility of Joyce's unpunctuated pages.
He is outraged. Where he expected to find a story
of love and ambition and struggle, he finds a bewildering crossword puzzle. And I am afraid that
he cannot be touched by the plea that Joyce has

achieved a masterpiece of modern subjective fiction, that he is a pioneer, breaking his way into strange, new fields of interpretation. He wants a story and that is the end of it.

But there are always a few who, from one motive or another, are willing to give more serious effort to the understanding of way-breakers, and it is for these that I have written this little book. I cannot pretend to understand all of *Ulysses;* it is to Joyce himself that one must look for a complete guide, a sure key to unlock the mysteries of this unique volume. But the outlines here set forth have enabled me to follow the thread of the narrative, the footsteps of the principal characters, and to make, for my own satisfaction, a sufficiently objective background against which the somewhat ghostly Dubliners may move in relief.

The major portion of this present essay was done in the spring of 1924. Since that time the Liffey has carried much water beneath Whitworth Bridge; and upon Mr. Joyce's life and work painstaking criticism has focused no inconsiderable light. Through the essays of Mr. Herbert Gorman, M.

INTRODUCTION

Valery Larbaud and Dr. Collins—to mention only a few—we have come to see that Joyce is no mere trifler with Gertrudesteinwayed words; no Greenwich-Village-Montmartre sensationalist, striving to astound the bourgeoisie; no manufacturer of privy-poetry for smart young intellectuals; but a sensitive, scholarly craftsman, a-search for a new way to record the secrets of the human soul.

I shall not here attempt to write even a biographical sketch of James Joyce; but because his books are so largely pieced out of his own life, because the Stephen Dedalus of *The Portrait of the Artist*, and *Ulysses* is, in the main, the author's own image, it is necessary to recall to the reader's mind, even at the risk of tedium, some of the more significant features of his career. And because this work has been more fully done elsewhere, and by more capable hands, I here take the liberty of summarizing those characteristics that seem necessary to an understanding of the second most important actor in *Ulysses*.

Bear in mind, then, these facts:

James Joyce is now (1927) forty-five years old.

That means that in 1904, the time of the story, he was just past his twenty-second year. He is a Dubliner, and knows his city thoroughly. His parents were Roman Catholics and he was saturated in a ritual and a theology from which he has achieved a mere intellectual emancipation. His instincts, his spiritual life, are still hungry for that to which his childhood and racial memories accustomed him. No more completely sundered and warring personality ever put pen to paper.

Joyce attended schoool at Clongowes Wood, a Jesuit institution, near Dublin. He received his degree from the Royal University in the city of his birth. Following his graduation, he studied medicine for a few years, but was dissatisfied and turned to the cultivation of his voice. (In *Ulysses* note, particularly in Chapter 15, how effectively the author makes use of medical terminology. His musical bent makes itself evident in nearly every chapter,—snatches of song, vocal exercises, and even a score intrude themselves everywhere.)

He is a linguist. He is familiar with Greek, Latin, German, Norwegian, and the Romance languages. He has taught in Trieste, Rome, Zurich and Paris.

The *Odyssey* has always been one of his favorite books, and, as a boy, we are told that he chose Ulysses for his hero. Dedalus, the name under which he masquerades in his two novels, came to him from Greek mythology. This mythic hero was artist, magician, maker of labyrinths, aeronaut, and exile. The name was not idly chosen.

Aside from his interest in Greek literature, we find that Joyce has been a close student of Tertullian, Thomas Aquinas, Dante, Shakespeare (one of his favorite themes is the problem of Hamlet in relation to the private life of Shakespeare), Elizabethan poetry, Dostoievski and Ibsen; the hairsplitting, logic-chopping of the Middle Ages; the passionate Italian extremists; the tragic side of Shakespeare; the dainty in poetic expression; Russian soul-surgery; Norwegian morbidity.

One might go far in cataloging the books that, at one time or another, have influenced James Joyce. I mention but the more obvious. But in the first chapter of *Ulysses* alone, we hear of Walt

Whitman, Oscar Wilde, the Mabinogion and the Upanishads.

In business, Joyce made two unsuccessful ventures,—an attempt to found a daily paper—which was to have been called "The Goblin"—and his brief experience with the "Volta" moving-picture house. Dr. Collins grows satiric over this last experiment, and professes to see in the jig-saw movement of the celluloid film an explanation for the Joyce technique.

Dr. Collins makes another statement which, it seems to me, is belied on every page of *Ulysses*. Speaking of Joyce's youth he says: "He lost his faith, and soon his patriotism, and he held those with whom he formerly worshipped up to ridicule, and his country and her aspirations up to contumely" (The Doctor Looks At Literature. Page 39).

Let us see: "He lost his faith"? Yes, perhaps, but not his instinct for faith; he escaped the priests, but not the Church: "and he held those with whom he had formerly worshipped up to ridicule"? Right, and I should be disposed to add *"malicious* ridicule." But for the rest,—"and soon his patriotism" and "his country and her aspirations up to contumely"—that seems the verdict, the diagnosis of myopia. The ready journalist got the better of the psychologist. Joyce obviously despises the sentimental, nose-dripping, bar-room-shouting patriot, the kind to which Dr. Johnson made sarcastic reference; but what sensible man does not? He curses Ireland because she has not lived up to her great men, has not been steadfastly loyal to the heroes who are sleeping in Glasnevin. Has Dr. Collins not heard of over-compensation?

When a man shouts his hatreds as loudly, as frequently, as hysterically as Joyce, the Psychologist begins to suspect that his "hate" is but a mask for love. So much for that. I have turned aside here for the reason that the issue rises in probably every extended conversation, and in nearly every chapter of *Ulysses*. Let the reader work it out for himself.

In *Ulysses* we find Stephen Dedalus at the National Library discussing Shakespeare-Hamlet (Chapter 9), just as Joyce did in his youth. The ash-plant cane of the novel was familiar to the students of the Royal University, and the impertinence of Dedalus was more than matched by that of his creator.

The experience, then, of Stephen, the teacher; Buck Mulligan, the medical student; of Mrs. Bloom, the singer, are familiar to Joyce. For that matter, the characters of *Ulysses* were Joyce's neighbors. Dublin is a city of some three hundred thousand people. It is Ireland in epitome; but it is also a village,—a whispering gallery of neighbors and a hot-bed of homely gossip. It is heated by religious discussion and political dissension. England stands (perhaps I should say "stood") as its particular devil, blocking that progress, that freedom of which its patriots dreamed. It is a thwarted, inhibited city of suppressed wrath. Its life, to the ardent idealist, has become mean and petty. It is the city of "dreadful night".

Joyce, feeling all this, lays bare its provincialism, its smallness, its hatreds, its racial animosities, its futilities, its street brawls, its sordid amusements, along with its more genial humors, and its pitiful inventions for escaping boredom. In part he has done his work with deliberate malice, but for the most he is but a psychologist, making analysis of perversions that are seldom set down in fiction.

I do not pretend to know why Mr. Joyce took for his modern Ulysses a Jew—Rudolph Bloom (alias Virag). The suggestion that a comparison of the wandering Jew with the wandering Ulysses may have influenced the author, seems remote and unsatisfactory. But there is one characteristic of this commonplace victim of auto-erotomania and lost manhood which, without a doubt, interested his maker—conscience troubled by home-sickness. Bloom had forsaken the god of his fathers. In this one thing, he finds kinship with Stephen.

To enjoy *Ulysses* one must first read *A Portrait of the Artist as a Young Man*. One is then prepared to follow Stephen through nearly seven hundred kaleidoscopic pages where, flea-like, he appears and vanishes. Furthermore, one must not skip a word. What is set down in the early chapters will reappear, possibly in fragmentary form, later. And one must be prepared not only to dog the footsteps of the flesh-and-blood actors in this drama, their speeches, their business; one must not be surprised when, in the midst of their conversations, stray bits of former speeches, memories, visions, associated ideas, intrude themselves. Strange creatures parade themselves in this labyrinthine volume. Bloom's scented soap; Hyam's Trousers; H. E. L. Y. S., the walking advertisement; Elijah, (an advertisement of the late Alexander Dowie), and Plumtree's Potted Meat.

Again, Bloom may hum a popular—and usually scandalous—ditty, in which, for example, the words "To keep it up" occur. Those words will bob up quite unexpectedly for the next ten pages, just as the blind man's uncanny tap-tapping does in Chapter 11.

These suggestions will not serve to explain the inner meaning of *Ulysses*, for every man will there find what he is able to find. But, if the reader will make use of the outlines here set down, he will be able to trace the thread of the narrative with ease, keep the principal characters and their action in mind, and, if so be *Ulysses* is a book for him, with the difficulties of the method thus simplified, he will get readily enough at the heart of the story.

NOTE

I have placed this brief outline of the *Odyssey* to the front that the reader may refresh his mind by recalling the principal events of the Homeric story. I do not hold, with M. Larbaud, that the *Odyssey* affords *the* key to *Ulysses*.† But since Joyce has evidently taken a good part of its frame-work, I take the liberty of giving this sketch.

†Note from the John Quinn Catalogue:

In the MSS of Ulysses occur these headings, made in Joyce's own hand: The first slip case contains: Part I: Telemachus, Proteus, Nestor. Part II: Calypso, Lotus Eaters, Hades, Eolus, Lestrygonians, Scylla and Charybdis.

The second slip case contains Part II continued: Wandering Rocks, Sirens, Cyclops, Nausikaa, Oxen of the Sun.

The third slip case contains Part II continued: Penelope, Ithaca, and Part III down to page 618.

I. OUTLINE OF THE ODYSSEY

"THE theme of the Odyssey," says Professor Palmer, "is the dominance of mind over circumstance." The story is twofold: The wanderings of Ulysses, a man seeking to return to his home, wife and son; the faithfulness and strategy of Penelope. A minor theme is the anxiety of Telemachus, the son, to recover his father.

Books I–IV. Telemachus

The Odyssey presupposes a knowledge of the fall of Troy, and the part Ulysses had in that great siege. After the fall, the heroes of war return to their homes, but Poseidon determines to delay Ulysses, and for this purpose disturbs the sea.

Ulysses is for seven years the captive of Calypso, who desires to marry him. But the goddess Athene intervenes in behalf of Ulysses, and encourages Telemachus to seek his father. To this end he obtains a ship and goes to the island where Nestor dwells, hoping from that friend to obtain news. Nestor knows but little, but he receives Telemachus kindly, makes him presents and sacrifices a heifer to his friendly goddess. Telemachus next visits the home of Menelaus who informs the lad that his father is on Calypso's island.

This much is but a prelude to the real story of the Odyssey. It gives us a picture of the son's state of mind, describes the ruin that is wrought by the one hundred and eight suitors for Penelope's hand,—suitors who hope to persuade her that her husband will never return, and who, meantime, eat her substance.

Books V–XIII. Wandering Ulysses

There are twenty-four books in all, and what is described above sums up but four. In Book Five, Mercury goes to Calypso, and bids her set Ulysses free. This she finally does, complaining that she is surely as good looking as Penelope. When Ulysses sets sail, Poseidon is enraged and stirs up a storm at sea, but Ino assists him and he manages to make the shores of Phaeacia. In Book Six, Nausicaa finds Ulysses naked on the shore, embarrassed and needy. She has him clothed and takes him to her father, King Alcinous. Here Ulysses is treated with the greatest respect, a banquet is given in his honor; he is entertained with games. His real name is unknown and he weeps when Demodocus sings in honor of Ulysses. Presents are showered upon him and he receives from the King a ship and fifty-two men to assist him home. In Book Nine, Ulysses discloses his name, and from then on until we come to Book Thirteen, he narrates his adventures. He tells how he landed on the island of the Cyclops; how he went, taking the name Noman, to the cave of Polyphemus, intending to get supplies; how this giant killed some of his men, and how he blinded him and made his escape back to the ships with the remainder of the crew. In Book Ten, we are told of the island of Aeolus, and of how Aeolus was kindly disposed, and of how he tied up all but the friendly West Wind; of how the Laestrygonians ate one of his men, and of how they escaped with but one ship; of how Circe turned his men into pigs, and of how he spent one night with her that she might release them; of how Elpenor was drunken and fell from the roof of Circe's house, breaking his neck; of how Ulysses was protected from Circe's spell by an herb called Moly, the gift of Mercury. In Book Eleven, Ulysses visits Hades where he sees the ghosts of Elpenor, of his mother, and of a number of others, including that of the blind prophet, Tiresias, who gives him counsel. In Book Twelve, Ulysses tells of the Sirens, of the difficulties of the floating rocks, Scylla and Charybdis, of the cattle of the Sun, and finally, of his stay with Calypso and his appearance in the domain of Alcinous.

Books XIII–XXIV. The Return

In Book Thirteen, it is related how the Phaeacians take Ulysses back to Ithaca, where Athene helps him to hide his valuable presents in a cave, and then fetches Telemachus. In Book Fourteen, Ulysses visits the hut of his faithful swineherd, Eumaeus, who feeds him, gives him goatskins to lie on, while he himself takes the skin of a goat for protection and goes out with his flocks. In the fifteenth book, Telemachus returns and finds his father at the hut of Eumaeus, but does not recognize him. In the sixteenth book, Ulysses makes himself known to him. In the seventeenth book, Ulysses, dressed as a beggar, goes to his own house unrecognized, and is ill treated by the suitors, who are in a hurry for Penelope to make a choice among them. Argus, the flea-bitten hound, knows him. Antinous, chief of the suitors, is most disagreeable to Ulysses. In Book Eighteen, Penelope makes the suitors give her presents; Ulysses fights as an insolent beggar. In Book Nineteen, Ulysses has a talk with his wife, who does not know him; is recognized by an old servant, whom he silences before she can betray his identity. In Book Twenty, the suitors continue to abuse him while their doom is prophesied; Penelope dreams during the night. In Twenty-one, there is the famous trial by bow, where

[31]

Ulysses alone strings the bow and sends an arrow through the handle-holes of the axes, to the dismay of the unsuccessful suitors. In Twenty-two, the suitors are slain by Ulysses and his son. In Twenty-three, Ulysses is recognized by his wife and friends, and he is received into his old room; next morning Ulysses and Telemachus go to the house of Laertes. In the final chapter, we see the ghosts of the suitors in Hades, and after Laertes has greeted his son, peace is made and all Ithaca is filled with content.

ULYSSES

PARTIAL CAST OF CHARACTERS

STEPHEN DEDALUS as *Telemachus*

LEOPOLD BLOOM as *Ulysses*

MRS. BLOOM as *Penelope*

BLAZES BOYLAN as *Antinous* (The Leading Suitor)

GERTY MACDOWELL as *Nausicaa*

MARTHA CLIFFORD as *Calypso*

PADDY DIGNAM as *Elpenor*

SKIN-THE-GOAT as *Eumaeus*

DAN DAWSON as *Eolus*

BELLA COHEN as *Circe*

THE MAD "CITIZEN" as *Polyphemus*

II. OUTLINE OF ULYSSES

BOOK I

CHAPTER I. Time: About 8:00 A. M., June 16, 1904. Place: Martello Tower, near Dublin. (pp. 3-23.)

Buck Mulligan, a medical student, is shaving. Stephen Dedalus and Haines, an Englishman, eat breakfast with Mulligan. Stephen's conscience is tormented by his conduct at his mother's death bed. Mulligan refers to Stephen's Greek name, and says (on page 7)* "together we might do something for the island—Hellenize it". On page 18, he announces that Dedalus is in search of a father; Stephen leaves the pair after breakfast to go to Mr.

---

*The page references are based upon the pagination in the first edition of *Ulysses*, Paris, 1922.

Deasy's school. In this chapter, Mulligan is Mercury, and, on page 17, so names himself.

* * * * *

CHAPTER II. Time: 9-10 A. M. (pp. 24-36.)

Opens with the question and answer of the school room. Mr. Deasy, who is here playing the part of Nestor to Stephen's Telemachus, gives Stephen his wages and asks him to have an article on hoof-and-mouth disease published. Stephen calls him the "Bullock-befriending bard". (Nestor sacrificed a heifer.)

* * * * *

CHAPTER III. Time: 10-10:30 A. M. (pp. 37-50.)

Stephen walks along the beach, meditating on his past, his mother, his school experience, the article in his pocket, his family and his loneliness.

* * * * *

BOOK II.

CHAPTER IV. Time: 8 A. M. Place: 7 Eccles Street. (pp. 53-67.)

Mr. Bloom (Ulysses), advertising solicitor for the *Freeman,* and an Irish Jew of Hungarian descent (real name Virag), sets about preparing breakfast for his wife, Marion Tweedy Bloom (Penelope). He goes out to purchase kidneys; on his return he brings in the mail,—a letter from his daughter, for himself; and, for his wife, a note from one Blazes Boylan (her lover and chief of the "Suitors"). After taking up breakfast to his wife, Bloom goes to stool, where he meditates and reads.

* * * * *

CHAPTER V. (pp. 68-83.)

Bloom to the postoffice in Westland Row where he receives a letter addressed to him as Henry Flower, from one Martha Clifford (Calypso). Thence he goes to mass at All Hallows (St. Andrew's) church; then to chemist's shop to have skin lotion prepared; buys a cake of soap; goes to public bath.

* * * * *

CHAPTER VI. (pp. 83-111.)

Bloom goes to interment of Patrick Dignam

(Elpenor) at Glasnevin Cemetery, passing Stephen Dedalus on the way; Bloom broods about the death of his only son, Rudy, who lived but eleven days; broods also upon his own father's suicide.

* * * * *

CHAPTER VII. (pp. 112-143.)

Bloom to office of Evening Telegraph (Cave of the Winds) about an advertisement for one Alexander Keyes. Technique changes in this chapter to reveal the atmosphere of modern newspaper office. Stephen Dedalus comes also to the Telegraph office, bringing the article written by Deasy. The editor advises Stephen to write about Dublin life (page 130), "Give them something with a bite in it. Put us all in." In the conversation, "A. E." and Madame Blavatsky are mentioned. Prof. Magennis speaks to Stephen about the sack of Troy (page 138); Stephen, Magennis and Myles Crawford go to Mooney's pub for a drink.

* * * * *

CHAPTER VIII. Time: About mid-day. (pp. 144-175.)

Bloom walks about Dublin; meets Mrs. Breen, who tells him of Mina Purefoy's coming accouchment. Goes to Burton's for lunch, but is disgusted by the manner of eating; leaves this for Davey Bryne's pub where he partakes of sandwiches and wine. Byrne and Nosey Flynn refer to Bloom's being a Mason, and of his caution in drinking. Bloom meets the blind piano-tuner and helps him across the street. He then proceeds to the Museum to look at nude statues.

* * * * *

CHAPTER XIX. (pp. 176-209.)

At the Library. Stephen dominates this chapter with his thoughts on Shakespeare, his loneliness, his egoism. The intellectuals of Ireland are pretty well represented: John Eglinton, Seumas O'Sullivan (here spoken of as "Starkey"), A. E. and several others. Padriac Colum, J. M. Synge, James Stephens are frequently referred to: Bernard Shaw, Frank Harris and Oscar Wilde are thrown in to reveal Ireland's contribution to Shakespearian criticism. Buck Mulligan interrupts with wild jokes and puns; also (on page 191) he plays the part of Mercury. On pages 187, 192 and 203, Ulysses is mentioned. In the conversation, Shakespeare is compared to Ulysses; Anne Hathaway to Penelope. On page 99, Stephen's rather wistful discourse on paternity, reveals the son in search of a father. Bloom appears on page 192, and again at page 209, where Stephen and he pass one another at the door. On this page, also, birds appear as messengers of the gods (as in the Odyssey).

* * * * *

CHAPTER X. *Place: All Dublin—and environs.* (pp. 210-244.)

A chapter broken into nineteen incidents occurring during the afternoon walk of Father John Conmee. 1. Conmee sets out, part by foot, part by tram, for the country. 2. Passes Corny Kelleher, the undertaker. 3. Mrs. Bloom flings an alms to one-legged sailor. 4. Katey and Boody Dedalus eat pea soup at home; Boody criticises her father. 5. Blazes Boylan purchases a basket of fruit for Mrs. Bloom at Thorton's. 6. Stephen takes a

walk with one Almidano Artifoni. 7. Miss Dunne,
a stenographer, notes the date (June 16, 1904),
and makes an engagement for Blazes Boylan with
Mr. Lenehan at the Ormond Hotel, 4:00 P. M.
8. Ned Lambert Exhibits the Council Chamber of
St. Mary's Abbey to a clergyman, Rev. Hugh C.
Love. 9. Tom Rochford, Nosey Flynn, M'Coy and
Lenehan are parting; M'Coy and Lenehan pass
Bloom at bookstall; later they pass Bloom's house.
10. Bloom looks at books, particularly Maria
Monk and Aristotle's work on Midwifery; he buys
"Sweets of Sin" for his wife. 11. Dilly Dedalus
meets her father and manages to get a shilling. 11.
Mr. Kernan meets Simon Dedalus, and together
they remember the death of Emmet, and his burial
at Glasnevin. 12. Stephen looks at a jeweller's
window, at a book-cart in Bedford Row (Bloom
has just preceded him here); Dilly meets Stephen
and shows him a penny primer she has purchased.
Stephen's conscience is troubled by her poverty.
14. Father Cowley meets Simon Dedalus, and tells
of his debts and of threatened attachment. 15.
Martin Cunningham works on a subscription for

the fatherless Dignams. 16. Mulligan and Haines see Parnell's brother, discuss Stephen's ideas of Shakespeare. 17. Artifoni walks down Holles Street and brushes against the blind boy whom Mr. Bloom assisted. 17. Master Patrick Aloysius Dignam buys a pound-and-a-half of pork steak, and soliloquises on death and his own importance as a mourner. 19. William, Earl of Dudley, (at that time Lord Lieut. of Ireland) and his wife drive forth in handsome carriage, drawn by well-shod horses; they pass most of the characters before mentioned.

* * * * *

CHAPTER XII. Time: 4:00 P. M. (pp. 245-279.)

Bronze-haired Miss Douce and gold-haired Miss Kennedy, Barmaids at the Ormond, hear the Earl's carriage go by; the effects of hoof-beats on the pavements, Bloom's fantastic thoughts, the gossip of persons at the bar, are expressed in a sort of chant; Lenehan enters the bar, and calls for Blazes Boylan. Bloom avoids Boylan, who shortly leaves for his appointment with Mrs. Bloom. This makes Bloom morose, but he partakes of liver, answers Martha Clifford's letter, muses on the fact that he is the last of his race and has no son (page 273); the blind piano tuner comes tapping his cane; music at the Ormond has curious effect on his meditations.

* * * * *

CHAPTER XII. (pp. 280-330.)

Joe Hynes goes to Barney Kiernan's to see the "Citizen". Alf Bergman sees the ghost of Dignam. Bloom is walking outside Kiernan's and is noticed and cursed by the "Citizen". Bloom comes in, refuses drink, takes a cigar; with the "Citizen" is an aged and flea-bitten dog called Garryowen. Then comes a rather silly parody on journalism and scientific jargon, to show the contempt of the crowd for Bloom's way of talking. Bloom argues with the "Citizen", then goes out to find Martin Cunningham. The crowd thinks he has gone to collect a racing bet. When he re-enters (page 326), argument is resumed, and Bloom defends the Jews. The

"Citizen" grows angry and hurls a biscuit tin at Bloom's head. Fortunately the sun blinds him and he misses. The "Citizen" bears some resemblance to Homer's Cyclops.

* * * * *

CHAPTER XIII. Time: 8-9 P. M. (pp. 331-365.)

Evening at Sandymount Beach.

Cissy Caffrey, Edy Boardman and the Caffrey twins, with Gerty Mac Dowell (Circe) enjoy the fireworks and the beach. Satiric picture of Gerty's mind, which has been fed on cheap romance. Bloom watches her. The children play about and the child mind is revealed. Children lose ball which Bloom recovers and throws so that it rolls beneath Gerty's skirt. Much is revealed as she gets the ball, and still more as she leans backward to watch fireworks. Bloom commits sin of Onan. The thoughts of the two are contrasted sharply, both in matter and manner. Bloom remembers the face lotion for his wife. The chapter ends appropriately with the notes of the Cuckoo.

* * * * *

CHAPTER XIV. Time: About 9:30 P. M. (pp. 366-407.)

A maternity hospital in Holles Street, of which Mr. A. Horn is head. Chapter opens with curious jumble of words indicating confusion, childbirth, reception of the new-born,—"Hoopsa boyaboy", etc. "Deshil" is probably a word from an ancient charm for infants,—Dessil. Bloom, Lynch, Madden, Punch, Costello, Mulligan, and Stephen are among those present. They drink and chatter. Bloom meditates on the death of his only son. Mrs. Purefoy brings forth her ninth child. Many parodies are here, Shakespeare, Mallory, Bunyan, Journalese, and finally one of modern evangelists.

* * * * *

CHAPTER XV. Time: 10:30-12:00.)

Mabbot Street, and the red light district, from about 10:30 till midnight. Conscience dominates fantasy. Bloom sees ghosts of his father and mother. The father reproaches him with loss of faith. The spirit of Bloom's living wife joins the

ghosts. Bloom makes excuses for himself for being
in this disreputable place; he supposes himself met
by a number of respectable persons. All his past
misdeeds and virtues unfold before him,—all his
past ambitions and dreams. The persons of the
fantasy, including himself, appear dressed and
environed as they were at the time of the memories.
There is a "Court of Conscience". The scene is
more particularized at the house of Bella Cohen,
82 Tyrone Street, where Stephen Dedalus and
Bloom meet. Stephen's dreams now appear along
with Bloom's. Bloom's grandfather; Stephen's
former plans about entering the church; Stephen's
reproachful mother. Private Carr enters the scene
with blasphemy. Stephen is drunk, and Bloom
takes care of him as the cloud of fantasy lifts.
Bloom looks upon Stephen as his charge and wishes
that he were his son. Ghost of Rudy Bloom appears, but the child does not recognize his father.

* * * * *

BOOK III.

CHAPTER XVI. *Time: Midnight till 1:00 A. M., June 17th.*

Bloom assists Stephen. There being no cab, and Stephen being in need of food and fresh air, they walk to cabman's shelter, belonging to Skin-the-Goat Fitzharris. En route they meet one "Lord" John Corley to whom Stephen gives a half crown. In the shelter they hold discourse with a sailor. Subjects of discussion are travel, the possibilities of Dublin, the city-cooped workingman, natural resources of Ireland, Bloom's wife, his exploits, Dignam's death, Jews, art, Parnell, etc. The coffee, Bloom notes, is distasteful to Stephen, so he proposes to take him to his home in Eccles Street where they will drink cocoa.

* * * * *

CHAPTER XVII. *Time: 2-3 A. M.*

Bloom's house. Dialectic method of treatment, by which Stephen and Bloom are compared and contrasted. The pair find it difficult to enter the house, since Bloom has forgotten his key. All of

Bloom's day is analyzed, his thoughts and posses-
sions are catalogued. Mrs. Bloom's (Penelope)
twenty-five suitors are enumerated; Bloom's ath-
letic prowess is mentioned. Stephen firmly refuses
to stay the night and passes out into the darkness.
Bloom continues his meditations, calls himself
"Noman" (page 679) as did Ulysses in the Cave
of Polyphemus, and at last goes to bed, where he
wakes his wife. Sleepy song ends the chapter.

* * * * *

CHAPTER XVIII.

Mrs. Bloom's earthy meditations, memories and
the outpourings of her subconscious. The story
descends to Earth.

III. INFORMAL COMPARISON

Ulysses, "a bald, middle-aged Greek gentle-man" (I quote Samuel Butler), is a patriot, but, setting aside the prejudices that must gather about a classic figure, an extremely human, eating, drinking, home-loving and erring mortal. For all his longing to go home, we find that he has light loves (even though these are at the command of the gods), is easily embarrassed, and is full of superstition, afraid of death, sees ghosts, has a conscience, is fond of recounting his deeds, dreams and failures. Also, he is afraid, at times, to tell his name, and even forgets to pay proper homage to the gods. Compared to Bloom in *Ulysses*, he is the essence of normality, and overcomes circumstances with greater ease. Yet, he too is thwarted by circumstance and cries out against fate. Penelope and Mrs. Bloom offer no essential comparisons, save in the matter of suitors. Mrs. Bloom succumbs with ease and pleasure. Her husband, also, has been absent for more than ten years, so far as normal conjugal relations are concerned (page 687). The Character of Telemachus is, again, unlike that of Dedalus except for the fact that he is fatherless, worried about his home and the laughing stock of his elders (the suitors). He is, as Samuel Butler notes, the virtuous young man defending his mother. But the whole theme, referring again to Prof. Palmer, is that of human wit overcoming obstacles. The dominant Ideas, according to Butler, are women, religion and money:

"The infatuation of man, with its corollary, the superior excellence of woman, is the leading theme," Butler continues (The Humour of Homer, pp. 77-78), "next to this come art, religion, and, I am almost ashamed to add, money. There is no love-business in the Odyssey except the return of a bald, elderly married man to his elderly wife and grown-up son . . . furious at having been robbed of so much money in the meantime. But this can hardly be called love-business; it is at the utmost domesticity. There is a charming, young princess, Nausicaa, but, though she affects a passing tenderness for the elderly hero of her creation . . . she makes it abundantly plain that she will not look at a single one of her flesh and blood admirers. There is a leading young gentleman, Telemachus . . . he has an amiable and most sensible young male friend. . . . Well, there is no lady provided either for this nice, young man or for Telemachus. . . . Two goddesses indeed, Circe and Calypso, do, one after the other take possession of Ulysses, but the way in which he accepts the situation . . . makes it plain that he does not care two straws. . . . Throughout the *Odyssey* the men do not really care for women, nor the women for men . . . Penelope, herself, who, on being asked by Ulysses on his return what she thought of him, said that she did not think very much of him, nor very little of him; in fact she did not think much about him, one way or the other. True, later on, she relents and becomes more effusive; in fact, when she and Ulysses sat up talking in bed and Ulysses told her the story of his adventures, she never went to sleep once."

Turning now to Joyce's story of *Ulysses*, we see that the first three chapters, or Book I, are made up of the meditations of Stephen Dedalus. They presuppose a knowledge of the ruin that has come upon his house (partly told in *The Portrait of the Artist as a Young Man*), and, in the speech of Buck Mulligan (Mercury) on page 18, it is indicated that Stephen is in search of a father. In Book II, that is from chapters 4 to 15, we are given the wanderings of Mr. Bloom. Death obsesses him. He attends the funeral of Patrick Dignam, and that death recurs to him constantly; also he is visited by ghosts: his father, mother, grandfather, son. He is hailed by sirens, Calypso (Martha Clifford) holds him. Nausicaa (Gerty MacDowell) both embarrasses and aids him at the seaside. He throws a ball to get her attention, just as, in the Odyssey, Nausicaa throws a ball to wake

Ulysses. The "Citizen" is angered by him, at Kiernan's, and, as a result, hurls a biscuit-tin at Bloom's head, just as Polyphemus hurls the top of a mountain at Ulysses. It will be recalled that in the Cave of Polyphemus, Ulysses calls himself "Noman." Dr. Collins has pointed out the fact that in the second phase of Bloom's argument with the "Citizen" Bloom is also nameless. And on page 679, Bloom applies the name "Noman" to himself. Bloom finally returns to his home with Stephen. At the cabman's hut (Skin-the-Goat), a sailor recalls the wonderful marksmanship (Ulysses was a distinguished marksman) of Stephen's father. Bloom has no key to his house, and therefore must enter in a surreptitious manner, even as did Ulysses. On entering bed, he wakes his wife who hears of his (somewhat expurgated) exploits. We are not told in the Odyssey whether Ulysses related his affairs with Calypso and Circe or not, but we may be sure, from Penelope's pleasant speech, that he did not.

As for the essential theme of *Ulysses*, it seems to be remorse of conscience, induced, in part, by death. Death is uppermost in the thoughts of the leading characters—Stephen and Bloom. If Butler is right about the *Odyssey;* if the leading ideas are man's infatuation, art, religion and money,—then surely there is a good basis of comparison. In the final solution, the meeting of father and son, Stephen and Bloom have, of course, only a symbolic relationship, but this is emphasized to the point, on page 565, where Bloom, standing over the drunken Stephen, is visited by the ghost of his own unseeing son.

I do not wish to push the comparison too far. Nor is it essential that it should be. Joyce has taken his favorite story for a frame-work and where that frame-work did not altogether suit him, he has made alterations. As to the detail, style and theme, his book is utterly different. The centuries that separate the two works are sufficient to explain. When the race was young, it was objective; now that it is weary and decadent, it is subjective.

If one wishes to go further in relating Joyce's book to Homer's, one may follow the criticism of Valery Larbaud, in *La Nouvelle Revue Française,* who writes thus of the episodes in *Ulysses*:

"Each episode treats of a science, or a particular art, contains a particular symbol, represents an organ of the human body, has a particular color (as in the Catholic liturgy), has an individual technique, and, in time, corresponds to one hour of the day.

"To be more explicit, let us take an example, episode 4 of the adventures. Its title is Eolus;—the place is a newspaper office, the hour, mid-day; the organ to which it corresponds, the lungs; the art of which it treats, rhetoric; its color, red; its symbolic figure, the editor-in-chief; its technique, enthymeme; its corresponding character, a person comparable to the Eolus of Homer; the incest compared to journalism, which is the Isle of the Winds; the death of Dignam to that of Elpenor."

It seems to me that this meticulous analysis adds little to the understanding of the book. That Joyce has taken his outline from the *Odyssey* is enough; his modernity, and his methods are so widely different that it is absurd to expect that he should have tried to make the stories fit in detail.

IV. ULYSSES—Agenbite of Inwit

BUDDHA, contemplating his wrinkled navel; orgiastic Pan, caressing the tender flanks of timid virgins; Baal, encrusted with the excremental offerings of his diarrhetic disciples; Jehovah, flinging liquid fire upon the naked consciences of tormented sinners; Dionysos, challenging Olympus with his inebriated corybants, who guzzle wine from the bleached-out skulls of their pious ancestors; nymphomaniacs, shrieking out the obscene commands of their insatiable lusts; necrophyles, playing with the rotting bowels of the dead; harpies, ensalivating the face of life with the contumelious tribute of an everlasting nay; blood-reeking surgeons of the soul, probing the quivering sub-conscious to lay bare the ultimate secret of its dreams; a Gargantuan Irishman, hurling riant blasphemies at the altars of God whilst his eyes yearn toward Golgotha;—out of such was made *Ulysses*.

Past all comprehension it is that despite all the hue and cry about this singular book, no one has the courage to come forward with an attempt to tell in just so many hard words what it is all about.* One detects in the critics of James Joyce either an adolescent and effervescing enthusiasm born of a yearning after the bizarre, or a middle-aged and pecksniffing fear of succumbing to a colossal literary hoax. Perhaps one should add that there is discernible among a few respectable critics a sort of snobbery begotten of a terror of the junk heap. One or two writers of pre-war repute have came mincing forward with mild huzzas deadened by the indistinct notes of a guilty reluctance. Men of forty are saying to themselves: this is all rot—and yet, and yet, it may be possible that it is the art of

*This was written prior to the appearance of Mr. Herbert Gorman's book on Joyce.

the future, and the next generation may rise up and call us super-asses; so here goes for a modern note of mild and qualified praise. I am perilously near this embarassing state myself. Still, the fact is that I approached this task with the full intention of setting forth the utter imbecility of *Ulysses*, and of taking up the cudgel in lusty defense of Paternian, Sirthomasbrowneian English. I have not abandoned my loyalties to the latter, but I have succumbed to the power and sweep of *Ulysses;* have come to reckon it one of the most significant books of this age. This change of front is due to the fact that I read the early and fragmentary chapters that appeared in the pages of the courageous *Little Review.* It is a mistake to read any novel in serial form, pulling at one's memory from month to month; it is impossible so to read *Ulysses.* Moreover, the influence of Joyce became immediately apparent in the writing of crack-brained, ill-informed moronettes, who, paying the tribute that mediocrity is said to yield to genius, aped the superficial mannerisms of their master, and thought to ride Pegasus without a bridle. Modernity came at a bound to mean poor spelling, no capitals, and the complete absence of punctuation;—bedlam in a psychopathic ward. One spits on the result.

But when one has spent a two weeks' continuous reading of the book itself, one is forced to a realization of its formidableness and of the essential genius of the author. Moreover, one finds that there is a story, compact, realistic and compelling. Once one is immersed in the thing, there is not a dull page or paragraph.

On the other hand, there is no book in the world —unless it be the *Anatomy of Melancholy*—that requires so much of the reader. To get a clear knowledge of the story, one needs to have read Mr. Joyce's other books—*Dubliners,* and, *A Portrait of the Artist as a Young Man.* One finds many of the minor characters of *Ulysses* in the short stories, and without the early history of Stephen Dedalus as set forth in the earlier novel, much in *Ulysses* is vague. In fact, it may be fairly said that *Ulysses* is but an extension and intensification of its predecessors. Besides these, one needs a good modern history of Ireland, a comprehensive essay on Dublin, Boyd's *Ireland's Literary Renaissance,* a copy of the Roman *Missal,* Latin, Hebrew, Greek, French, Italian, Spanish, Gaelic, English, and Medical Dictionaries, Grose's *Dictionary of Buckish Slang, University Wit and Pickpocket Eloquence,* Frazer's *Golden Bough,* Handbooks of Astronomy, Astrology, Theosophy, and Psychology, and a certain familiarity with modern Shakespearian criticisms; then, and not until then (if one does not skip a single word of the seven hundred and thirty-two pages), one finds in *Ulysses* one of the most fascinating stories ever set down on paper.

The English itself has to be translated; what seems at the first glance to be mere jargon turns out to be a coherent and very human story sounding the profound depths of our pitiful souls.

A bare outline of the tale will convey nothing of its power and interest, but it is necessary, nonetheless, in sustaining the thesis that there is a continuous narrative, to set down a skeleton of the action.

The book is divided into three sections, the first being devoted to Stephen Dedalus, setting forth the changes that have come about since we first made his acquaintance in *The Portrait of the Artist,* and the remorse that he has suffered from having refused to pray at his mother's death-bed. Some of the finest writing in the book is contained in these fifty pages. The second introduces Mr. Leopold Bloom, advertising solicitor 'and an Irish Jew, in the act of getting breakfast for his wife, and carries him through nearly one day of his life, compressing therein about a hundred years of Dublin history in six hundred and twenty pages. The third section—sixty-three pages—is given to the homeward pilgrimage of Mr. Bloom and Stephen Dedalus, to their visit in the kitchen of the Bloom residence, to Bloom's meditations on retiring, and, finally, to Mrs. Bloom's remarkable bedroom soliloquy. The events of this strange narrative occur in the space of nineteen hours on the Thursday-Friday of June the sixteenth and seventeenth, 1904.

Stephen Dedalus is suffering from what Joyce chooses to call "agenbite of inwit"*—remorse of

*Literally the "again-biting" of the inner wit. In this

conscience, and his feelings are in nowise alleviated by the brutality of his companion, Dr. Buck Mulligan, who opens the book with a flourish of his shaving brush. After a fantastic breakfast, with Hamlet's ghost and bawdy songs to provide the requisite cabaret atmosphere, Stephen sets forth to his daily task of teaching the children of Mr. Garrett Deasy. Accompanying him on this walk, as indeed everywhere, is the reproachful shade of his mother and the echo of an unsaid prayer:— "Liliata rutliantium te confessorum turma circumdet; jubilantium te virginum chorus excipiat,"—a crowd of blushing confessors surround you; a chorus of singing virgins receive you. The schoolroom scene provides an excellent opportunity for

connection it may be of interest to note that this phrase was once used as the title of a book by a Canterbury monk in the year of 1340:—*The Ayenbite of Inwyt*, by Dan Michel, is one of the early and important Mss. books of the transitional period of English literature, and is preserved in the British Museum. Its theme, as might be expected, is homiletic, and, among other things, it deals at some length with the seven deadly sins.

a pedagogical satire. After the lessons are done, Stephen receives from his employer the modest sum of three guineas, and is commissioned to carry an effusive article on the hoof-and-mouth disease to the Evening Telegraph. Dedalus calls Mr. Deasy "The Bullock-befriending Bard." En route to the discharge of Mr. Deasy's errand, Stephen loiters for a time by the seaside where he broods on the dark tragedies of life, beholds a dead dog—and some other things.

By far the greater part of the book is concerned with the doings of Mr. Bloom, the workings of his conscience, his ambitions, complexes, vocabulary, scientific attainments, schemes, amours, mnemonic system, appetites, prejudices, petty vices. The actions of this singular gentleman are simple enough. He prepares breakfast for his indolent stay-a-bed wife; reads a letter from his daughter; carries a mysterious message from the same mail to Mrs. Bloom, who hastily secretes the same; purchases a pork kidney for himself; feeds the cat; performs, with great enjoyment and profound meditation, certain necessary functions of nature; goes to the postoffice where he receives a letter from Mrs. Martha Clifford, addressed to him as "Mr. Henry Flower," attends mass, visits a chemist's shop for a face-lotion and a cake of scented soap, (which soap, by the way, becomes one of the leading minor characters in the book); enters a public bath; goes to the funeral of Patrick Dignam; attends to his duties at the newspaper office; meets Stephen Dedalus and some friends; stops at a public house; assists a blind piano tuner; saunters into a museum, where he gazes upon marble nudes; overhears a discussion on Shakespeare at the National Library; browses at a book stall over semi-erotic books, finally purchasing a copy of *The Sweets of Sin,* as sufficiently vulgar literature for his wife's consumption; sees, and makes the fitting gestures to the Earl of Dudley; lunches; answers Martha Clifford's letter; takes a free cigar in a public house; sees Miss Gerty MacDowell at the beach, with rather curious results to both; talks and drinks at a maternity hospital in Holles Street, while Mrs. Mina Purefoy brings forth a child; revels solemnly and sorrily in the shady side of Dublin; and, finally, assists Stephen Dedalus to his home where they partake of Epp's Cocoa, dissect the cosmos, perform again certain functions of nature; after which, parting from his friend and guest, he goes to bed. All of which is as common-place as a chapter from *Main Street*.

And that, briefly, is a sketch of the objective action. But it doesn't begin to tell the story, for, in spite of the fact that the work is mainly composed of meditations, that the arena is the human skull, it is full of the most violent action—street fights, brawls, stews, political, racial and religious altercation, intrigues and executions.

One learns the entire history of Mr. Bloom; of his father—who changed his name from Rudolph Virag to Rudolph Bloom, and, finally, after an unsuccessful career, committed suicide—; of his grandfather; of his wife, who was born in Gibraltar, daughter of Major Tweedy, who had distinguished himself at Plevna; of Mrs. Bloom's success as a singer, her failure as wife and mother, and her art of presenting several sets of horns to her husband; of Dublin's politics, her churches, the doings of her priests and preachers, her water supply, parks, burying grounds and streets; of her prostitutes; her poor, her rich, and of the small talk of her middle classes; Joyce has given, in fine, as much of the factual, intellectual and spiritual history of Dublin and its inhabitants in this one book as Balzac managed to give of Paris in his entire *Comedie Humaine.*

It would be unwise to look too closely into the question of why Mr. Joyce named his book for the hero of the *Odyssey,* for when one presses the analogy, it seems to make *Ulysses* a burlesque of Homer. Still, there are analogies, ridiculous as many of them are. Ulysses Bloom has his Nausicaa; tells of his wayfaring; has bitter experiences with Aeolus; meets Circe, and is transformed; visits the land of the dead; beholds strange ghosts; comes between Scylla and Charybdis; suffers from mistaken identity; enters his home after the manner of a beggar—by climbing over the garden wall—; is wounded (then there is a chapter devoted to the signs and wonders of his house); exhibits his prowess by having excelled on the parallel bars;

enumerates the suitors who have come to his wife. That, I think, is a fair sample of the likeness.

Mr. Joyce invents a variety of methods in telling his story,—each chosen for a particular purpose. For example, Mrs. Bloom's soliloquy is written without punctuation, her association of ideas is loose, extremely illogical, and highly absurd. The manner itself is sufficient to tell the reader that Mrs. Bloom is garrulous, ignorant and damnably annoying. The one thing in her favor is that she is never for a moment dull. In her, Joyce has created a masterpiece. I wish it were possible to quote from her meditations.

Again, there is the chapter relating to Mr. Bloom's hour at the *Evening Telegraph* office. To create a journalistic atmosphere, apt headlines are suddenly thrust at one in the midst of a confused medley of thoughts, sounds, and mental images. The turmoil of the average newspaper office was never set forth to better advantage. The conversations in the editorial rooms run along about gossip, advertising, news, politics, accompanied by the thump of presses and the click of typewriters.

Composers try to concentrate their thoughts upon the correct spelling of a word, while their fellows shout into nicotine-stained telephone receivers. Into the thick of this mumbo-jumbo come such headlines as:

NOTED CHURCHMAN AN OCCASIONAL CONTRIBUTOR

or

SOPHIST WALLOPS HAUGHTY HELEN SQUARE ON PROBOSCIS
SPARTANS GNASH MOLARS
ITHACANS VOW PEN IS CHAMP

In one of his most fascinating chapters, Joyce uses the Socratic method of question and answer in order to compare the mental attitudes of Dedalus and Bloom, to make contrast between the scientific and the artistic. Bloom—the scientific—dominates, with the result that the chapter is a torrent of scientific phraseology. For example, when Bloom prepares the cocoa for his guest, there comes, after a long disquisition upon the nature of water, and upon the value of heat, this question and its bewildering answer:—

"What concomitant phenomenon took place in the vessel of liquid by the agency of fire?

"The phenomenon of ebullition. Fanned by a constant updraught of ventilation between the kitchen and the chimney flue, ignition was communicated from the faggots of precombustible fuel to polyhedral masses of bituminous coal, containing in compressed mineral form the foliated fossilized decidua of primeval forest which had in turn derived their vegetative existence from the sun, primal source of heat (radiant), transmitted through omnipresent luminiferous diathermanous ether. Heat (convected), a mode of motion developed by such combustion, was constantly and increasingly conveyed from the course of calorification to the liquid contained in the vessel, being radiated through the uneven unpolished dark surface of the metal iron in part reflected, in part absorbed, in part transmitted, gradually raising the temperature of the water from normal to boiling point, a rise in temperature expressible as the result of an expenditure of 72 thermal units needed to raise one pound of water from 50° to 212° Fahrenheit."

The saturnalian, night-town scene is done in the form of a fantastic play, in order that the ghosts which disturb Bloom's conscience, together with the various personalities into which, at one time or another, he has merged himself may masquerade in the most compelling and terrifying manner. Moreover, the appalling stage directions permit the introduction of miscellaneous trappings that might otherwise be impossible to indicate. At one point, Leopold Bloom, here the potential politician and saviour of his country, is the center of a celebration. The stage directions for this scene read as follows:

"(A cannon shot. The man in the mackintosh disappears. Bloom with his sceptre strikes down poppies. The instantaneous deaths of many powerful enemies, graziers, members of parliament, members of standing committees, are reported. Bloom's bodyguard distribute Maundy money, commemoration medals, loaves and fishes, temperance badges, expensive Henry Clay cigars, free cowbones for soup, rubber preservatives, in sealed envelopes tied with gold thread, butter scotch, pineapple rock, *billets doux* in the form of cocked hats, ready-made suits, porringers of toad in the hold, bottles of Jeyes' Fluid, purchase stamps, 40 days' tickets available for all tram lines, coupons of the royal and privileged Hungarian lottery, penny dinner counters, cheap reprints of the World's Twelve Worst Books: Groggy and Fritz (politic), Care of the Baby (infantilic), 50 Meals for 7/6 (culinic), Was Jesus a Sun Myth? (historic), Expel that Pain (medic), Infants Compendium of the Universe (cosmic), Let's All Chortle (hilaric), Canvasser's Vade Mecum (journalic), Loveletters of Mother Assistant (erotic), Who's Who in Space (astric), Songs That Reached Our Heart (melodic), Pennywises's Way to Wealth (parsimonic). A general rush and scramble. Women press forward to touch the hem of Bloom's robe. The lady Gwendolen Dubedat bursts through the throng, leaps on his horse and kisses him on both cheeks amid great acclamation. A magnesium flashlight photograph is taken. Babes and sucklings are held up."

Every method Joyce brings to his work is patently for the purpose of analyzing the stream of consciousness, of tracing it, so far as possible, to its source; for unmasking all the hidden fears and hopes, shames and prides over which respectability has hung its etiolated fig-leaves, and concerning which, cowardice has created its canting camouflage. It is the most powerful technique yet devised for stark photographic realism. The brain-clogging delusions of time and space have been waved aside by this Irish metaphysician. He is enabled to set down not only what his characters would naturally say, but also, and at the same time, what they would think, and why they would think it. A man says a certain thing because of the way his grandfather drank, of the way his mother died, of what he, at the time, tastes, smells, sees, remembers or fears. And when a man utters a word, the machinery of association is set to work, resulting in such jumblings as:—

"—Grandest number on the whole opera, Goulding said.

"——It is, Bloom said.

"Numbers it is. All music when you come to think. Two multiplied by two divided by half is twice one. Vibrations: chords those are. One plus two plus six is seven. Do anything you like with figures juggling. Always find out this equal to that, symmetry under a cemetery wall. He doesn't see my mourning. Callous: all for his own gut. Musemathematics."

At first sight, one is at a loss to understand the opening sentences of the chapter dealing with the maternity hospital on Holles Street, where a company is assembled to await the accouchement of Mrs. Purefoy,—the astounding:—"Deshil Holles Eamus. Deshil Holles Eamus——Hoopsa, boyaboy, hoopsa! Hoopsaboyaboy, hoopsa!"—is very puzzling. The thing is silly enough in all conscience until one finds that "Deshil" comes from an old charm for the protection of mothers and infants, and that "Holles Eamus" is merely a proposal to go into Holles Street where the maternity

hospital is located. Still, the "Hoopsa, boyaboy,"
seems idiotic. But when one reflects that this is
merely a prelude to the bringing forth of a male
child, it seems fitting enough. When you call to
mind the conduct of fathers upon the advent of a
son, I believe that you must admit that the introduction fits itself admirably to the state of mind.

Just here, however, one must call a halt. The
paragraphs immediately following this outburst
are unconditionally inept and unpardonable. Wit-
ness:—

"Universally that person's acumen is esteemed
very little perceptive concerning whatsoever matters are being held as most profitably by mortals
with sapience endowed to be studied who is ignorant of that which the most in doctrine erudite and
certainly by reason of that in them high mind's
ornament deserving of veneration constantly main-
tain when by general consent they affirm that other
circumstances being equal by no exterior splendour
is the prosperity of a nation more efficaciously as-
serted than by the measure of how far forward
may have progressed the tribute of its solicitude for

that proliferent continuance which of evils the original if it be absent when fortunately present constitutes the certain sign of omnipollent nature's incorrupted benefaction."

Here it is possible to so rearrange the words as to make out that scientific and sanitary devices should be employed to insure the health of mothers and children; that a nation failing to interest itself in these matters is stupid. But merely to arrange words in the form of a Chinese puzzle is pointless. It is unfortunate that Mr. Joyce has chosen to commit this folly so many times in a work of such significance. Here also it may be pointed out that he has overworked the atrocious habit of punning; nearly all his characters are guilty of this to an extent entirely out of keeping with their natures. Another stupid blunder may be illustrated by the following, which occurs in the famous Socratic section, comparing Stephen and Bloom:—

"Did they find their educational careers similar?

"Substituting Stephen for Bloom Stoom would have passed successively through a dame's school and the high school. Substituting Bloom for

[76]

Stephen Blephen would have passed successively through the preparatory, junior, middle and senior grades of the intermediate and through the matriculation, first arts, second arts and arts degree courses of the royal university."

Comment is unnecessary, the paragraph is preposterous. One may, of course, discern in this, after a study of the context, that Bloom wishes he were in Stephen's shoes, but the effort required to decipher such passages is not justified.

Joyce's ability to set forth the essential characteristics of his creatures through their meditations is little short of miraculous. The contrast of the temperaments of Leopold Bloom and Gerty MacDowell is a case in point. The average novelist would have described Miss MacDowell's sentimentalism in an objective fashion with no such power as is achieved by her own day dream of the seaside-strolling Bloom. Bloom appears on the scene by chance and comes before her, looking sad and lonely, whereupon she feels that he is her long-looked-for knight:—

"She saw the magic lure in his eyes— . . . She

would make the great sacrifice. Her every effort would be to share his thoughts. Dearer than the whole world would she be to him and gild his days with happiness . . . Heart of mine! She would follow her dream of love, the dictates of her heart that told her he was her all in all, the only man in all the world for her, for love was the master guide. Nothing else mattered. Come what might, she would be wild, untrammeled, free . . . She knew that he could be trusted to the death, steadfast, a sterling man, a man of inflexible honor to his finger-tips." Then Mr. Bloom:—"Mr. Bloom watched her as she limped away. Poor girl! That's why she's left on the shelf and the others did a sprint. Thought something was wrong by the cut of her jib. Jilted beauty. A defect is ten times worse in a woman . . . Glad I didn't know it when she was on show. Hot little devil all the same. Wouldn't mind."

The vocabulary of *Ulysses* is a delight. One can see at a glance that Joyce is no mean student of philology. Also, he has a trick of word combination derived from a thorough saturation of Greek

literature:—"Woodshadows," "Wavewhite wed-
ded words", "Dewsilky cattle", "Milkoozing
fruits", "The heaven-tree of stars hung with humid
nightblue fruit"; or, in another vein—"Bootjack-
manufacturer". But here also he lapses into folly:
—"Velvet mantletrimmed with ermine" is fearful
rot, and "Contransmagnificanjewbangtantiality" is
execrable. Indeed many of Joyce's devices are
bad, and his analyses of thought-content could
in many places have been better expressed by
ordinary regard to punctuation and conventional
form. And it is here of course, that he will have a
most evil influence. Literary fledgelings will seize
upon his absurdities with passion, just as they have
mimicked the worst of Walt Whitman. Not until
a careful and discriminatory work of elimination
shall have been undertaken by a considerable number of serious technicians can the remarkable ex-
periments of James Joyce exercise that beneficent
and revolutionary influence indicated in nearly
every section of his book. When this has been ac-
complished it will be found, I am persuaded, that
this startling Celt has not merely added new weap-

ons, but a complete new arsenal to the realistic school of fiction.

On every page there are sentences that stick in one's mind:—"Irish art is the cracked looking glass of a servant", "History is a nightmare from which I am trying to awake". I pick these at random. But there is one sentence by which I am sure Joyce would like his work to be tested, and by which test this book is sure to take its place among the masterpieces of the modern world:—"The supreme question of a work of art is: Out of how deep a life does it spring?" One may be sure, after a careful perusal of *Ulysses* that it came out of the great deeps of the life of an extraordinary scholar who has chosen to lay bare his very soul.

The book is, however, by no means all serious. It abounds in hoaxes, rollicking nonsense, and great good humor. And there are more parodies and burlesques in these pages than in any other book I know. Shakespeare, Whitman, Malory, and Bunyan are parodied in the same merciless manner as Madame Blavatsky, Irish journalism, and the Dublin Mystics. And he has done this in no banal manner; they constitute some of the most amusing sections of his work. The most blasphemous of these is the parody on the Apostle's Creed, relative to the British navy:—

"They believe in rod, the scourger almighty, creator of hell upon earth and in Jacky Tar, the son of a gun, who was conceived of unholy boast, born of the fighting navy, suffering under rump and dozen, was scarified, flayed and curried, yelled like bloody hell, the third day he arose again from the bed, steered into haven, sitteth on his beamend till further orders whence he shall come to drudge for a living and be paid."

Bloom in the red-light district imagines himself met by respectable folk. He imagines defences, imagines the overthrow of the defences, imagines himself persecuted for his conduct; has illusions of grandeur, followed immediately by a debased wallowing in the very pits of humility. These dreams of his are modified by the opinions of others, and the results of his imagining are thus parodied. For example:

The Veiled Sibyl

(Enthusiastically) I'm a Bloomite and I glory in it. I believe in him in spite of all. I'd give my life for him, the funniest man on earth.

Bloom

(Winks at the bystanders) I bet she's a bonny lassie.

Theodore Purefoy

(In fishing cap and oilskin jacket) He employs a mechanical device to frustrate the sacred ends of nature.

The Veiled Sibyl

(Stabs herself) My hero god! *(She dies)*

(Many most attractive and enthusiastic women also commit suicide by stabbing, drowning, drinking prussic acid, aconite, arsenic, opening their veins, refusing food, casting themselves under steamrollers . . . asphyxiating themselves in stylish garters, leaping from the windows of different storeys.) "

A little later, where Bloom's character is receiving burlesque defence from Dr. Dixon:

"Professor Bloom is a finished example of the new womanly man. His moral nature is simple and lovable. Many have found him a dear man, a dear person. He is a rather quaint fellow on the whole, coy though not feebleminded in the medical sense. He has written a really beautiful letter, a poem in itself, to the court missionary of the Reformed Priests Protection Society which clears up everything. He is practically a total abstainer and I can affirm that he sleeps on a straw litter and eats the most Spartan food, cold dried grocer's peas. He wears a hairshirt winter and summer and scourges himself every Saturday. He was, I understand, a firstclass misdemeanant in Glencree reformatory . . . I appeal for clemency in the name of the most sacred word our vocal organs have ever been called upon to speak. He is about to have a baby.

Bloom

O, I so want to be a mother.

Mrs. Thornton

(*In nursetender's gown*) Embrace me tight, dear. You'll soon be over it. Tight, dear.

(*Bloom embraces her tightly and bears eight-male yellow and white children . . .*)"

Deadly satire there is—wholesome and tonic, and as applicable to America as to Ireland. There is, for instance, Bloom's election speech: —

"I stand for the reform of municipal morals and the plain ten commandments. New worlds for old. Union of all, jew, moslem and gentile. Three acres and a cow for all children of nature. Saloon motor hearses. Compulsory manual labor for all. All parks open to the public day and night. Electric dishscrubbers. Tuberculosis, lunacy, war and mendicancy must now cease. General amnesty, weekly carnival, with masked licence, bonuses for all, esperanto the universal brotherhood. No more patriotism of barspongers and dropsical imposters. Free money, free love and a free lay church in a free lay state . . . "

After Bloom has made this characteristically pompous political speech—which the Lord Mayor so heartily favors that he orders it printed at the expense of the rate payers,—motion is made and carried that "the house in which he was born be ornamented with a commemorative tablet and that the thoroughfare hitherto know as Cow Parlour off

Cork Street be henceforth designated Boulevard Bloom". There is great applause from the populace, much fireworks, and a long procession passes beneath the triumphal arch. Bloom is strongly approved for several minutes, due to the influence of leading citizens and his own blarney. Then rises Alexander J. Dowie with this disconcerting speech:—

"Fellowchristians and antiBloomites, the man called Bloom is from the roots of hell, a disgrace to christian men. A fiendish libertine from his earliest years, this stinking goat of Mendes gave precocious signs . . . vile hypocrite, bronzed with infamy . . ."

The Mob:—

"Lynch him! Roast him!"

At this juncture, medical evidence is brought forward.

Doctor Mulligan:—

"Dr. Bloom is bisexually abnormal . . . Traces of elephantiasis have been discovered among his ascendants . . . Ambidexterity is also latent. He is prematurely bald . . . a reformed rake, and

has metal teeth . . "
        Doctor Madden:—
"Hypsospadia is also marked. In the interest
of coming generations I suggest that the parts af-
fected should be preserved in spirits of wine in the
national teratological museum."
        Doctor Crothers:—
"I have examined the patient's urine. It is al-
buminoid. Salivation is insufficient, the patellar
reflex intermittent."
        Doctor Punch Costello:—
"The *fetor judaicus* is most perceptible."
    This entire chapter is made up of noble non-
sense, a tissue of remarkable day-dreams—of what
Mr. D. H. Lawrence would call fantasia of the
unconscious—, a further exposition of Bloom's remorse of conscience, his inferiority complex, his
abysmal fears, and his compensating delusions of
magnificance.
    By far the greatest value of the work lies in its
keen analysis of our grotesque mental processes.
Mr. Bloom suffers alternately from secret delusions
of grandeur and a base inferiority complex. He is

oppressed by the thought of being a Jew:—

"What, reduced to their simplest reciprocal form, were Bloom's thoughts about Stephen's thoughts about Bloom about Stephen's thoughts about Bloom's thoughts about Stephen?

"He thought that he thought that he was a jew, whereas he knew that he knew that he knew that he was not."

Most delicious of all is the manner in which Mr. Bloom appeases his sense of sin in approaching the problem of sex relationship by comparing this act with other little sins in the following manner:—

"As natural as any and every natural act of nature expressed or understood executed in natured nature by natural creatures in accordance with his, her and their natured natures of dissimilar similarity. As not as calamitous as a cataclysmic annihilation of the planet in consequence of a collision with a dark sun. As less reprehensible than theft, highway robbery, cruelty to children and animals, obtaining money under false pretences, forgery, embezzlement, misappropriation of public money, betrayal of public trust, malingering, mayhem, corruption of minors, criminal libel, blackmail, contempt of court, arson, treason, felony, mutiny on the high seas, trespass, burglary, jailbreaking, practice of unnatural vice, desertion from armed forces in the field, perjury, poaching, usury, intelligences with the king's enemies, impersonation, criminal assault, manslaughter, wilful and premeditated murder. As not more abnormal than all other altered processes of adaptation to altered conditions of existence, resulting in a reciprocal equilibrium between the bodily organism and its attendant circumstances, foods, beverages, acquired habits, indulged inclinations, significant disease. As more than inevitable, irreparable."

In no book has there been such a frank disclosure of secret masculine meditation; of those delectable moments spent on the close-stool, paying tribute to Cloacina and contemplating the metaphysical mysteries of the universe; of one's thoughtful picking at the nostril, or scrutinizing unguinal fragments at the bedside. Or, on the other hand, what an exposure of the feminine libido there is in Madame Bloom's Rabelaisian soliloquy! Nor must one forget Martha Clifford's subtle endeavors to discover the favorite perfume of her paramour's wife!

Ulysses can have no universal appeal; its reading is too formidable a task for that; but as a writer's source book, it is an inexhaustible mine of strange treasures, a veritable encyclopedia of the human soul, and a song of ecstacy. But it does bear a universal message—a weird cry from the very depths of Dublin to the rim of the world—, the cry of tortured conscience, "agenbite of inwit."

Vulgar it is, certainly,—as vulgar as a bed pan, as vulgar as life itself. But it is relieved by moods of singular beauty; it swings one from the stinks of the lavatory to the realms of luminous ether. It is everything: realism and romanticism, wisdom and nonsense, scatologic hideousness and transcendental aspiration.

And, finally, alas, there has probably never been a book, since the invention of printing, doomed to exert such a baneful, such a malignant and perverting influence as *Ulysses*. It is the Demogorgon of literature.

CITY LIGHTS BOOKS

Artaud, Antonin ANTHOLOGY
Beck, Julian THE LIFE OF THE THEATRE
Bly, Robert THE TEETH-MOTHER NAKED AT LAST
Bowen, Michael JOURNEY TO NEPAL
Bowles, Paul A HUNDRED CAMELS IN THE COURTYARD
Bukowski, Charles ERECTIONS, EJACULATIONS, EXHIBITIONS AND GENERAL TALES OF ORDINARY MADNESS
Bukowski, Charles NOTES OF A DIRTY OLD MAN
Burroughs, William & Ginsberg, Allen THE YAGE LETTERS
Cassady, Neal THE FIRST THIRD and Other Writings
CITY LIGHTS JOURNAL (No. 3)
Corso, Gregory GASOLINE
Corso, Gregory THE VESTAL LADY ON BRATTLE
Cossery, Albert MEN GOD FORGOT
Daumal, René MOUNT ANALOGUE
David-Neel, Alexandra SECRET ORAL TEACHINGS IN TIBETAN BUDDHIST SECTS
di Prima, Diane REVOLUTIONARY LETTERS, ETC.
Dowden, George BIBLIOGRAPHY OF ALLEN GINSBERG
Ehrlich, Dr. Paul ECO-CATASTROPHE
Fenollosa, Ernest THE CHINESE WRITTEN CHARACTER AS A MEDIUM FOR POETRY
Ferlinghetti PICTURES OF THE GONE WORLD
Genet, Jean MAY DAY SPEECH
Ginsberg, Allen AIRPLANE DREAMS
Ginsberg, Allen THE FALL OF AMERICA
Ginsberg, Allen HOWL AND OTHER POEMS
Ginsberg, Allen INDIAN JOURNALS
Ginsberg, Allen KADDISH AND OTHER POEMS
Ginsberg, Allen PLANET NEWS
Ginsberg, Allen REALITY SANDWICHES
Hemingway, Ernest COLLECTED POEMS
Journal for the Protection of All Beings No. 2 ON THE BARRICADES
Journal for the Protection of All Beings No. 3 GREEN FLAG: People's Park Poetry
Joyce, James POMES PENYEACH
Kaufman, Bob GOLDEN SARDINE
Kerouac, Jack BOOK OF DREAMS
Kerouac, Jack SCATTERED POEMS
Lamantia, Philip SELECTED POEMS
Leary, Timothy EAGLE BRIEF
Lowry, Malcolm SELECTED POEMS
Mailer, Norman THE WHITE NEGRO
McClure, Michael MEAT SCIENCE ESSAYS
Michaux, Henri MISERABLE MIRACLE
Moore, Daniel BURNT HEART
Mrabet, Mohammed M'HASHISH Trans. Paul Bowles
O'Hara, Frank LUNCH POEMS
Olson, Charles CALL ME ISHMAEL
ON THE MESA: Anthology of Bolinas writers
Parkinson, Thomas PROTECT THE EARTH
Patchen, Kenneth LOVE POEMS
Patchen, Kenneth POEMS OF HUMOR & PROTEST
Picasso, Pablo HUNK OF SKIN
Pickard, Tom GUTTERSNIPE
Plymell, Charles LAST OF THE MOCCASINS
Pommy-Vega, Janine POEMS TO FERNANDO
Prévert, Jacques PAROLES
Rexroth, Kenneth (Tr.) THIRTY SPANISH POEMS OF LOVE & EXILE
Richards, Charles & Janet CLASSIC CHINESE & JAPANESE COOKING
Sanders, Ed POEM FROM JAIL
Smith, Paul Jordan A KEY TO THE ULYSSES OF JAMES JOYCE
Solomon, Carl MISHAPS, PERHAPS
Solomon, Carl MORE MISHAPS
Svevo, Italo JAMES JOYCE
Topor, Roland PANIC
Upton, Charles PANIC GRASS
Voznesensky, Andrei DOGALYPSE
Waley, Arthur THE NINE SONGS: A Study of Shamanism in Ancient China
Watts, Alan W. BEAT ZEN, SQUARE ZEN AND ZEN
Whitman, Walt AN AMERICAN PRIMER
Williams, William Carlos KORA IN HELL: IMPROVISATIONS
Wilson, Colin POETRY & MYSTICISM
Winslow, Pete A DAISY IN THE MEMORY OF A SHARK
Yevtushenko, Voznesensky & Kirsanov RED CATS
Yevtushenko, Yevgeni FLOWERS & BULLETS